BIJNI KINGDOM

SENIOR GENERAL

Contents

Preface

This book deals with the history of the Bijni Kingdom. Hope that the publication of this book will be useful. This book may not be free from errors and constructive criticisms are welcomed for the improvement of this book.

CHAPTER I

Introduction

The **Bijni Kingdom** was the estate in possession of the Bijni family, descended from the Koch general Chilarai, of the Koch dynasty from 1534 to 1584. After the division of the Koch kingdom in 1584 into Koch Bihar and Koch Hajo Raghudev established his capital at Barnagar in the Barpeta (now a district in Assam), and received as his share the Koch territories lying to the east of Sankosh River.

After the death of Nara Narayan in 1584, Raghu Rai declared independence. The eastern kingdom ruled by Raghu Rai came to be called Koch Hajo and the western Koch Bihar. Soon after the declaration of independence, the two kingdoms started displaying hostilities against each other. Raghu Rai was succeeded by his son Parikshit Narayan and was defeated in 1602 by the army of Nawab of Dhaka (governor for the Mughals) who was moved by Lakshmi Narayan (ruler of Koch Bihar). Parikshit was defeated at Dhubri (now a district in Assam) and sued for peace. But soon, he continued with the hostilities and in 1614 was driven up to Pandu, now in Guwahati. There, Parikshit surrendered and agreed to become a vassal of the Mughal Empire. But before he could take up this assignment he died. The Mughals then appointed Kabisekhar as the kanungo and instructed Sheikh Ibrahim Karori to set up a Mughal system of administration. Parikshit' son Bijit Narayan, was confirmed by the Mughals as 'jamindar' of the area between the river Manas and the Sankosh, and from him the Bijni family descended. The name "Bijni", now a sub-division of Chirang district of

Bodoland Territorial Area in Assam, comes from the name of the king Bijit Narayan.

Under the Mughal rule, the Bijni king Bijit Narayan paid a tribute of Rs. 5,998 which was afterward commuted to an annual delivery of 68 elephants. During the last two decades of the 17th century, the Mughals lost their influence on Assam while the East India Company gradually started strengthening their foothold in different parts of India including Bengal.

The East India Company was awarded the 'diwani' or overlordship of Bengal by the empire following the Battle of Buxar in 1764 and the company came to an agreement (known as Permanent Settlement) with Bengali landlords in 1793 to fix revenues to be raised from land. With the Treaty of Yandaboo in 1826, the East India Company finally took control of the both Eastern Assam and Western Assam. However, it was doubtful whether Goalpara was ever included in the Permanent Settlement. According to *The Imperial Gazetteer of India* (Volume 8), a small assessment from the Bijni kingdom was always accepted in lieu of land revenue, though it has sometimes been argued it was nothing more than a tribute. The Imperial Gazetteer of India, which was published in 1902, states that the Bijni family paid a revenue of Rs. 1,500 and cesses amounting to nearly Rs. 19,000 for an estate which covered an area of 950 square miles (2,500 km^2) with an estimated rent-roll of Rs. 2 lakh.

On the conclusion of the Bhutan war (or Duar War) fought between British India and Bhutan in 1864–1865, the Bijni family put forward claims to hold a large tract of land in the Eastern Duir which they alleged that they were in possession under the Bhutan government. The claim was admitted and in 1870 a settlement was effected with the

Court of Wards on behalf of the minor Bijni Raja. The present extent of the estate to which they were entitled was still matter of uncertainty, but in 1882 it was ruled by the government of India that the Raja should receive 130,000 acres (530 km^2) of land. These estates generally remained under the direct management of the government, who allowed to the Raja 7.5 percent of the collections as his share of profits.

CHAPTER II

Archaeological Monuments

Ram Rajar Garh near Deohati village is a man-made historical pond which was excavated by Ramsingh I of Ambar Kingdom of Rajasthan. Ram Singh had the pond excavated during the Mughal campaign (Battle of Saraighat) against the Ahom kingdom.

The **Lalmati-Duramari Ganesh Temple** near Abhayapuri, is one of the oldest temples in Assam. The historical authenticity of the images are yet to be ascertained. Based on the study of the stone carvings and modes related to the carved idols, some archaeologists has opined that the temple and images belong to 8th to 10th centuries AD. The existence of ruins in Lalmati-Durgamari area along with temples was brought to the notice of the Historical & Antiquarian Department of the Govt. of Assam in 1974. The department undertook excavation work which resulted the discovery of the temples, images and idols of Gods and Goddesses.

The **Lungai Pahar Shiva Temple** is located 10 km away from the main town of Abhayapuri. Visitors need to climb the 227 stairs to reach the temple inside which there are stone carvings of Lord Shiva, Lord Ganesha and Goddess Kali.

CHAPTER III

People and Culture

Since time immemorial, Koch-Rajbonshies (belong to Indo-Mongoloid ethnic group of people) have been living in this area now known as Abhayapuri. These people are the original sons of the soil and their existence can be traced back to the "Kiratees" of pre-vedic epic age (Mahabharata). These Kiratas of dim past are also mentioned in Kalika-Purana and Yogini Tantra and also in histories written both by native and foreign scholars.

Yogis, Kalitas, Kayasthas and older Muslims are also indigenous who settled in this part of land prior to the advent of Britishers in North East Region. Some of them settled in the area centuries before the advent of Britishers. In a much later period, people from different parts of Assam migrated to Abhayapuri.

Major festivals such as Diwali, Holi, Durga Puja, Swaraswati Puja, Lakshmi Puja, Kalipuja and Shivaratri are celebrated by the Hindus of Ahbayapuri. Those of Islamic faith celebrate Idd and Muharram. Besides the religious festivals, Bihu, the agricultural festival of Assam is celebrated by all Assamese, irrespective of caste, creed or religion.

The people of Abhayapuri have long been known for their interest in culture and education. The 44th conference of The Asam Sahitya Sabha was held in Abhayapuri in 1977 under the presidency of Syed Abdul Malik, a big name in the history of modern Assamese literature. The area where the conference was held is still known as **Sahitya Sabha Path** (Road).

CHAPTER IV

Abhayapuri

Abhayapuri was the third capital (after 1897) of the Bijni kingdom that was established by king Bijit Narayan alias Chandra Narayan in 1671. Bijit Narayan was the son of Parikshit Narayan who was the grandson of Sukladhwaj alias Chilarai, the Koch general and the younger brother of Nara Narayan, the ruler of Koch dynasty of Kamata Kingdom in the 16th century.

The first capital of Bijni kingdom was located at modern Bijni town (1671–1864), but it was later shifted to Dumuria (now known as Dalan Bhanga) when attacked by Jhawlia Mech and (a local chief under Bhutan Kingdom). The Assam earthquake of 1897 disfigured the royal palaces of Dumuria which led to the Queen Abhayeswari Devi (the widow and second queen of Raja Kumud Narayan Bhup Bahadur) who was the then ruler of Bijni to shift the capital to the Deohati forest area which was later renamed as Abhayapuri after Devi Abhoyamata, the family deity of the ruling dynasty. In 1956, during the rule of Raja Bhairabendra Narayan, the kingdom officially joined the Union of India.

CHAPTER V

Rulers of Bijni Kingdom

- Bijit Narayan (alias Chandra Narayan)
- Joy Narayan
- Shiv Narayan
- Bijoy Narayan
- Mukunda Narayan
- Haridev Narayan
- Indra Narayan
- Amrit Narayan
- Kumud Narayan
- Abhayeswari Devi
- Jogendra Narayan
- Bhairabendra Narayan.

References

Bukumar. V. (2013). Social Exclusion and Ethnicity in North-East India. The NEHU Journal. Vol. XI, I-2, pp-19-35.

Col Ved. P (2007). Encyclopedia of North-East India. Atlantic Publishers and Distributors Pvt. Ltd; New Delhi. Vol. 5.

Rao,V. V., Hazarika. N (1983). A Century of Government and Politics in North-East India. S. Chand and Company Pvt. Ltd; New Delhi. Vol. I.